The King's Confessor

A Play by Martin Thrush

The King's Confessor
A Play by Martin Thrush

Edited with Introduction
by Kris Christopher

SENEX
PRESS

The King's Confessor: A Play by Martin Thrush
Copyright © 2025, The Martin Thrush Literary Estate
All rights reserved.

No part of this book may be reproduced in any form or by an electronic or mechanical means, including artificial intelligence technologies and information storage and retrieval systems, without written permission from the author or press, except for the use of brief quotations in a book review or article.

Senex Press
Boston, Massachusetts
www.senexpress.org
"We publish the best books."

For Dick Christopher

"Let's be sacrificers, but not butchers, Caius."
~*Julius Caesar*, Act 2, Scene I

"Who doesn't wish for his father's death?"
~Ivan, *The Brothers Karamazov*

Contents

Introduction – The Darkling Thrush
   by Kris Christopher i

Dramatis Personae x

Act I 1

Act II 25

Act II 59

Epilogue 75

A Word from the Editor-in-Chief 79

Introduction
The Darkling Thrush

There is no remembrance of former things, sayeth the preacher, neither shall there be any remembrance of things that are to come with those that shall come after. A mercy, I think, in most cases, justice, in more—but true in all. Martin Thrush, the playwright, the madman, the world-historic genius, has only been dead for half a century and already his memory has evaporated with the snows of yesteryear. Once upon a time, he was regarded as a kind of oracle, the keeper of Apollo's secrets, the only living man who knew what was to come after the death of modernism and the disintegration of its corpse (or what is now known as "post-modernism"). He was, to the cognoscenti, the hidden king of two continents and a two-thousand-year literary tradition. And now it is as if he never was.

Even at the apex of his fascination and influence, he was more shade than man, more half-heard rumor than flesh and blood. His oeuvre, as far as we can tell, comprises three completed plays, only one of which has ever been published, and the entirety of his biographical details could fit on a baseball card. In his lifetime and after, there was hardly more than a name, but it was a name that bowed heads from one

Cambridge to the other. Why that came to be the case is a matter of extensive debate. No one denies that it was through Robert Lowell that Martin Thrush was first introduced to the rarefied circles of literary culture. But where they met, and the result of that meeting, is decidedly more controversial. Some say it was in 1943, at the West Street jail in Manhattan, where the poet laureate was being held before his transfer to federal prison in Danbury, Connecticut for refusing to serve in World War II, on the grounds of his Catholic faith. Others insist they met at one of Lowell's several visits in the 1950s to McClean Mental Hospital in Belmont, Massachusetts to treat his intermittently fulminating bipolar disorder. (Any hope of consulting the records of either the West Street jail or McClean have long ago been lost to fires and floods and neglect.) Far from some matter of scholarly pedantry, the answer to this riddle is extremely significant. While there is something of a consensus that *The King's Confessor* was the work that bowled the famously discerning and contemptuous Lowell over, how it impacted him seems to depend on the proper dating of this first meeting.

Those who insist on the West Street rendezvous credit Thrush, more than T.S. Eliot or Allen Tate, for the baroque mysticism of *Lord Weary's Castle*. In particular, these scholars claim that it was Thrush's impenetrable St. Vincent that hurled Lowell into the angelic possession that birthed his first masterpiece. Lowell officially converted to Catholicism in 1941, devastating his Boston Brahmin parents, whose relations still had the chisel from Plymouth Rock, with such an emphatic renunciation of his inheritance. He anointed himself with oils and other superstitions of the European refuse that had lately washed up on the banks of the hub. How much of this conversion was out of genuine religious conviction or simply animus towards his parents is hard to say. In any case, he applied himself to the old faith with the industry of a clinically diagnosed maniac. He was a daily communicant. He said not one, but two rosaries a day. He tried to hector indigents that he encountered on the street into conversion with such adamance and tactlessness that he was eventually stabbed and briefly hospitalized. And yet, for all of this energy and fervor, he could not complete his much-awaited first volume of poetry. That would not happen until after his stay in prison. Lowell has been quoted, more than once, with saying that there was a time when he could only hear Christ's voice when St. Vincent spoke. This obscure remark (which no one has sufficiently unriddled) has been taken by the partisans of the West Street encounter as proof that Thrush's play was the inspiration for his best and most mystical Catholic poetry. They claim that *The King's Confessor* was the occasion for a second conversion: from a performative, hollow faith to a genuine infatuation with the God who became man.

Interestingly, the advocates of the McClean meeting come to the polar opposite conclusion. They believe it was Mr. Thrush and his play that ultimately convinced Lowell to surrender his devotion to Rome. The evidence for this interpretation can be found in the laureate's celebrated poem "Beyond the Alps," where he laments his inability to accept the dogma of Mary's assumption into heaven:

> The lights of science couldn't hold a candle
> to Mary risen—at one miraculous stroke,
> angel wing'd, gorgeous as a jungle bird!
> But who believed this? Who could understand?

Scholars argue that this objection could be the epigraph for Thrush's play. The disconsolate King, as he confesses so movingly at the end, wants very badly to surrender himself to Christ's absurdity, but he cannot. As Lowell says (and King Louis might as well have), "Much against my will / I left the City of God where it belongs." Far from showing Lowell the way to a true faith, these scholars argue, *The King's Confessor* proved to him that he could never have it.

But it was not only Lowell who was dramatically altered by his encounter with Thrush. Some scholars have claimed that Lowell's dear friend Elizabeth Bishop began her 15-year sojourn in Brazil as a fortnight visit with Martin Thrush, at Lowell's urging. Apparently, Thrush summered like some 19th Century Brazilian emperor in Petropolis, just outside of Rio. Lowell claimed that this was because the playwright could only write in a Catholic city, and there wasn't another one in this hemisphere. Saul Bellow insisted it was because he gifted Thrush a copy of *The Posthumous Memoirs of Bras Cubas*, which sent him off immediately to "pray at the shrine of Machado de Assis." Allen Ginsberg demurred that it was in fact because Thrush preferred Brazilian prostitutes, who were "irresistibly exotic to a bookish twerp from the boroughs, who understood just enough Portuguese to confuse their desperation for enthusiasm." Whatever the actual reason, we know that Thrush spent some twenty-five summers or more in the shadow of Christ the Redeemer's outstretched arms, where he hosted a handful of the most innovative writers of the century. In an interview for *Playboy* in 1970, Borges reflected, with mingled admiration and melancholy, "For me, Italo [Calvino], and Gabriel [Garcia Marquez], Thrush was to the new world and the second great war what Ezra Pound was to the old and the first—or rather, he should have been."

Thrush has disappeared from the history of letters, much as he disappeared from the historical record in 1962—abruptly, seemingly irrevocably. That fateful summer, he traveled down to his second, adopted, preferred home and then, like Ambrose Bierce, walked off into oblivion. The search for him was not extensive. In the first place, he was famously reclusive, with a Schopenhauerian desire for silence and solitude. While he was, like most of his writer contemporaries, a binge drinker of herculean proportions, and while he clearly enjoyed, provided he was sufficiently lubricated, the company of those he found amusing or pleasing to ridicule, he liked his own company and that of his typewriter best. It was not unusual for him to neglect correspondences or phone calls for weeks or months at a time. He had a habit of exiting functions, cities, time zones without an excuse or even a word. Secondly, he had no concerned family, no devoted and inquiring public, and no friends, outside a handful of writers and academics—all of whom, I think, were a little embarrassed of his influence on them, glad of his obscurity, and tired of fearing his manic outbursts, which could be terrifyingly violent. (He was remanded to the West Street jail in 1943 for throwing a gentleman down a flight of stairs for talking too loudly and too long outside the door adjacent to his desk; he found himself in McClean for defacing the Robert Gould Shaw monument with a knife because he "refused to tolerate the colonel's ignoring [him] so imperiously from that horse.") His friends, such as they were, however they might deny it, were somewhat relieved to be rid of him. I know at least my father was.

The venerable Dr. Christopher met Martin Thrush when they were both scrawny undergraduates. Randomly assigned roommates, if I remember correctly, they were an odd pair. The sullen Martin "Don't-call-me-Marty" and the gregarious Richard "But-call-me-Dick" could not have been less suited for one another. And yet, for all of their obvious incongruities, they remained friends all the way through to graduation and for many years afterward, mostly at my father's insistence. Dick's nickname was much more appropriate, let's say, than he liked to let on, and I think he enjoyed a kind of vicarious release when Marty (he was one of a handful of men who could call him that) unseamed some luckless victim from the nave to the chops. But even more than that, I suspect my father knew that he was in the presence of genius, and it was his great fortune, and pride, to recognize it before anyone else. For Marty's part, I think he sensed my father's admiration and respected him enough to take some pleasure in it. If there was more to his reciprocal affection than that, I never saw it, but of course, in his insolent pride he would never show it.

Unsurprisingly, perhaps, this unlikely love affair did not have a happy conclusion. As is customary in foundered relationships, each party leaves with his own calamitous finale. For my father, the *coup de grâce* was my baptism, which my should-have-been godfather did not show up for, or even offer any excuse for missing. My mother, whatever indignation she tried to feign, was delighted that the twice-arrested, arrogant prick would be out of her daughter's life and hers, and much more than that that she was right—she knew this would happen, and she had said so. Dick, on the other hand, was shattered. He had hoped that Marty's newly discovered religiosity would make him, if not a better man, at least a better friend. As he admitted later, he was an idiot for thinking so, and he could not say what was harder to forgive, the slight itself or the exposure of his ingenuousness—ultimately, he forgave neither.

In a 1948 edition of *The Mixes Nate Review*, my father wrote a bilious take-down of *The King's Confessor*, then being staged off-off-Broadway in the basement of a rundown Episcopal church. He deemed it a "failure in every conceivable sense" and then proceeded to methodically disassemble the play, scornfully regarding every aspect, only to leave a heap of refuse:

> As a drama, it is tedious beyond endurance, lacking not only a plot but even characters. Louis, Vincent, Mazarin, and Queen Anne are as flat and derivative as the paper they are printed on. As historical fiction, it is obscenely and gratuitously inaccurate. To pick just two of the distortions: King Louis did not die at Christmas but Easter, and his confession was not some kind of existentialist navel-gazing soliloquy, but according to St. Vincent himself, one of the most moving and sincere displays of piety he ever witnessed. What reason, what possible excuse, for such license, such slapdash application of a well-attested historical record? I wonder if Mr. Thrush ever asked himself the question. Finally, and most appallingly, I must say, as a work of art, of an individual artist who stamps his name and reputation on the title page, it is a shameless, brazen plagiarism. Almost all of the third act is almost a line-for-line rendering of scenes from the Academy Award-winning film *Monsieur Vincent*. One should at least wait until such an artistic and commercial success has faded somewhat from the popular imagination to rifle through its treasures. I suspect one will not have to wait very long to safely pillage *The King's Confessor*. Like any scrap heap, it is not without its trinkets. There

are, to be fair, a few amusing epigrams that I'm sure Mr. Thrush is very proud of. But even these are spoiled by the wooden (and for some reason British) English diction, which is intermittently doused with some spittle of the Gallic tongue about as sophisticated as the ejaculations of Pepé le Pew. *Pourquoi? Je ne sais pas.* I suppose it must be because Mr. Thrush has little French, and less sense.

A postcard arrived in due course from Petropolis. It read: "Thank you for confining your tantrum to such an obscure publication. If you had stuffed it in a bottle and hurled it into Boston Harbor, it would have found more readers. As ever, you are a true friend." The image on the front was Marty laughing with Borges on a balcony in Rio.

Until the day my father died, he insisted that he was right in his assessment of *The King's Confessor*, however personal, and unbecoming, his motivations may have been in publishing it. He felt supremely vindicated that it never attracted any public or critical notice. But I know that it bothered him immeasurably that Uncle Marty was able, nonetheless, to attract such consequential friends and establish such a mythical reputation, without him, almost in spite of him. That's why he accepted it without any skepticism when Lota claimed that Martin drowned himself in Guanabara Bay, even though there was no note and no other evidence to support it, even though, at the time, she was in a psychiatric hospital against her will, and as we would later understand, wrestling with her own plans for suicide. Like any scorned lover, Dick wanted to believe that Marty, however stubbornly he tried, and however convincingly he played the part, could not in fact live without his only true friend, his other, more charming, more successful, less talented and less tortured self.

How could I possibly turn down the opportunity to edit the recently excavated plays of Martin Thrush when so much personal and literary history is tangled up in these scant pages? It is a service that I owe to my father, my sometime godfather, and the broader public of letters, which for too long has profited from this forgotten master's influence without hearing his inimitable voice. *Venez, écoutons.*

K.C.
July 19th, 2025
Formerly the Feast of St. Vincent de Paul

The King's Confessor

Dramatis Personae

Vincent de Paul . . . . The Priest
Cardinal Mazarin. . . . . The Prince
Louis XIII . . . . The Fool
Fool . . . . The Philosopher King

Act I

I.1 *A windswept road. Enter Leper shaking his bells.*

LEPER
Alms! Alms for a poor sinner!

Enter a carriage and its Driver.

DRIVER
Allons-y![1] Be gone with you!

LEPER
Alms! For a sinner in need!

DRIVER
Allons-y! Out of the road before I come down there!

LEPER
Alms! Alms!

DRIVER
Fils de pute![2]

Enter Vincent de Paul from carriage.

VINCENT
What's this?

DRIVER
Rein, monsieur l'abbé.[3] A little obstacle. A trifle. Get back in the coach. We'll be moving again in a minute.

---

1 Let's go!
2 Son of a bitch!
3 Nothing, Father.

LEPER
Alms! Alms!

DRIVER
I said out of the road, cretin! Now get out of here! We're riding *pour le roi*.[4] I have license to do what's needed to ensure safe travel.

VINCENT
Just a minute. Cold night, *mon frère*. What's your name?

DRIVER
Revenir. Get back in the coach, *l'abbé*. Let me handle this.

VINCENT
What's your name, *mon ami*?

LEPER
Alms! Alms for a sinner?

VINCENT
It's too cold to be traveling this road alone. Why don't you join us?

LEPER
Alms? Alms?

---

4   ... for the king.

VINCENT
We'll make a short detour. There's a mission house not far from here, right next to the Saint-Germain parish. We can drop him there for the night.

DRIVER
We'll do no such thing. The Cardinal ordered me to take you straight to the Château and I aim to do it.

VINCENT
The Cardinal can afford to wait.

DRIVER
Revenir. Get back in the coach, *l'abbé.*

VINCENT
I intend to. And to take our new friend here with me.

DRIVER
I won't be late for the Cardinal.

VINCENT
You will. Or you'll arrive on time without your passenger.

DRIVER
Monsieur l'abbé!

VINCENT
Take us to the mission or I'll walk this man there myself. Ready the horse.

LEPER
Alms!

VINCENT
Allez. It's freezing out here.

Exeunt omnes.

I.2 *A château at Christmastide. Enter Cardinal Mazarin and Queen Anne.*

MAZARIN
I wouldn't expect too much from this country priest, my lady. It's hard for any of us to understand the plight of a king, let alone one who lives at such a remove from court and the affairs of the crown.

ANNE
He may surprise you, *Éminence*, as he has so many others.

MAZARIN
Surely you don't believe the stories?

ANNE
And why not? What little faith you have... for a man of God.

MAZARIN
If what they say is true, then he's a living saint.

ANNE
Is there no such thing anymore?

MAZARIN
I wouldn't go so far as to call myself an unbeliever...

ANNE
God forbid.

MAZARIN
I'll just say that in my four decades on this earth, I've yet to meet one.

ANNE
How do you explain his converting those riotous nobles?

MAZARIN
How I explain most human things, my lady: Calculated self-interest.

Enter Vincent.

MAZARIN
Welcome to the home of our Royal Sovereign, *monsieur l'abbé*. I know His Majesty is eager to meet you.

Observing a Christmas tree.

MAZARIN
A contemptible custom. I told His Majesty that it was invented by that reprobate Luther and that no respectable Catholic would engage in such ignoble practices.

ANNE
I'm afraid my husband is ... Well, he's a simple man.

MAZARIN
He insisted that decorating trees is *"amusant."*

ANNE
You see, *monsieur l'abbé*, His Majesty means well. He's a beneficent king. But as all of France has come to know, good intentions don't necessarily yield good results.

MAZARIN
This way, if you please.

They walk to a crowded hall. Enter revelers and Fool.

MAZARIN
I'm not sure why he insisted on seeing you, *monsieur l'abbé*. He seems to have gotten it into his head that you're some sort of healer. Not that he's unwell, but... His stomach ails him, and he has trouble sleeping at night.

ANNE
We were hoping that you might have a word with him. He doesn't listen to us. The only man he's ever trusted was Richelieu. But with him gone... How to say it?

MAZARIN
The king isn't getting younger, Father. And ever since the death of my predecessor, he's developed a bit of a morbid disposition. We wouldn't share this if we weren't certain that he's going to tell you himself but... The king is worried that he might be dying. He's not of course. Nothing could be further from the truth. At this age, his father had another fifteen

years in him. But His Highness won't listen when I tell him that. In fact, he's dismissive of much of my good counsel.

ANNE
The thing is, *monsieur Vincent* (may I call you *monsieur Vincent?*), he likes you already. Even though he's never met you, still he likes you, just based on what he's heard. That's the way with him. Simple. But he can be an obstinate man as well.

FIRST REVELER
Give us some advice, sage!

SECOND REVELER
Yes, but no jesting! Impart your true wisdom.

FOOL
It's wisdom you seek?

Cheers.

FOOL
All right. How's this?

Love not the comforts of the bed
Lest by mistake you make a grave.
Love not the wisdom of the head
Lest being wise, forsake the knave.
Love not sweetmeats
Nor crisp, chilled wine
Lest you retreat from man to swine.
But if you're after the divine,
Then order life as I do mine:

> With whore and harlot on each arm,
> Adorned in scarlet, filching alms,
> With words of honey for each king
> And sword and money, emerald ring,
> Parade about the continent
> Bedecked in jewels and ornament,
> Spewing Christian love and hope
> And soon enough, they'll make you—Pope!

Applause and laughter.

FOOL
Now there's the God's truth,
if ever it's been uttered!

Enter the Dauphin.

DAUPHIN
Maman! Maman!

ANNE
Salut, mon amour!

MAZARIN
Father, allow me to introduce you to
Louis Dieudonné, Dauphin.

VINCENT
I think I have one. Yes, here we are.

He takes a coin from his pocket and hands it to the boy.

VINCENT
Have you ever heard the story of St. Nicholas of Myra? He lived a long, long time ago in a far-off land called Asia Minor, a place now ruled by the Turks. He loved children and always gave them lots of gifts. One Christmas, he heard of a poor family who had no money for their daughter's dowry. Without it, they knew she would never marry and would live in destitution all her life. Do you know what St. Nicholas did? He devised a plan to get them the money without anyone knowing it. He waited until everyone was fast asleep. Then he climbed up on their roof and snuck down their chimney with a bag of gold coins. He hid it in a pair of the daughter's stockings, and when she found the gold the next day, she gave it to her parents who used it for her dowry. She married a good man and lived a happy life, and no one ever knew where the blessing had come from.

ANNE
How wonderful!

MAZARINE
Almost beyond belief.

VINCENT
Avez-vous faim?[5] Here, let me see that coin. There are two lessons here, my child. First, never boast of your good deeds. The God who sees in secret knows what you've done, even if the eyes of the world remain blind to it.

---

[5] Are you hungry?

He unwraps the coin and gives the boy the chocolate hidden inside.

VINCENT
Second, don't be deceived by the glint of gold.
Always check what's behind it.

ANNE
Génial!

MAZARIN
I shudder to think what would become of a king who cared for neither honors nor riches.

He bows to the boy.

MAZARIN
If you'll follow me, *monsieur l'abbé*, His Majesty is waiting.

FOOL
Nuncle! Leaving us so soon, nuncle?

Laughter.

MAZARIN
Out of our way, knave!

FOOL
Why do you abuse me, nuncle? Are we not brothers, you and I?

MAZARIN
We are no such thing.

FOOL
We both advise the king.

MAZARIN
One of us advises and one makes a mockery of his court.
FOOL
You're more self-aware than I thought!

More laughter.

MAZARIN
I said step aside.

FOOL
Which side would you have me step, nuncle?

MAZARIN
Stop calling me that! You don't even know what you're saying, you abominable wretch. Nuncle is what the fool calls the king in the play.

FOOL
Are you not he, my lord? I thought "king" was the name given the man who shares the queen's bedchamber!

Gasps.

MAZARIN
I will have your tongue!

FOOL
My tongue, like my life, belongs to His Majesty.
And you just told us that you are not he.
Though we all know you would be!

Mazarin hurls the Fool.

MAZARIN
My apologies, *monsieur l'abbé*. As you can see, the court has devolved in recent months, what with the king's ailment and his welcoming of scoundrels to his table.

FOOL
I fall today, nuncle. And you tomorrow. That's the only difference between us, fool and fool!

ANNE
My husband's judgment has been impacted by his affliction, *monsieur Vincent*. His morbid outlook has led to a number of improprieties. We need someone to talk to him, someone he will listen to, someone he respects. Things can't go on like this. He's inviting rebellion.

Exeunt.

I.3 *King's chambers. Louis reposes. A knock at the door.*

LOUIS
Oui! Bien! J'ai besoin de plus de vin![6]

---

6   Yes! Good! I need more wine!

Enter Mazarin.

MAZARIN
C'est moi, Majesté.

LOUIS
Ah. You. What is it?

MAZARIN
I've brought your guest, my lord.

LOUIS
Guest? I didn't call for a guest. I called for more wine!

MAZARIN
Do you remember, my lord? You asked me to bring you monsieur Vincent de Paul. He's the country priest everyone's been talking about.

LOUIS
De What? Speak up, Mazarin, you louse! You know I'm hard of hearing.

MAZARIN
De Paul, Your Highness. The priest who they say converts the proud and cares for the lowly. You made him chaplain to the galleys?

LOUIS
De Paul? De Paul? Ah. De Paul.

MAZARIN
Yes, my lord. Shall I send him in?

LOUIS
No, I think not.

MAZARIN
You don't want to see him, my lord?

LOUIS
No. Will that be all, *Monseigneur*?

MAZARIN
Oui, Majesté. Désole.

Exit to outer chamber where Vincent and Anne await.

MAZARIN
Je suis désole, monsieur l'abbé.[7]
Apparently, His Majesty isn't up to having
any visitors this evening.

ANNE
But surely—
MAZARIN
Perhaps we can try again in the morning.

VINCENT
I have to return to my work at the galleys.

ANNE
But it's past nightfall.

---

7   I'm sorry, Father.

VINCENT
Misery doesn't sleep, my lady.

MAZARIN
Stay the night, *monsieur l'abbé*. I know His Majesty would appreciate it.

VINCENT
I really ought to go. The morning comes early and there's much to do.

MAZARIN
Tell me, *l'abbé*. Haven't you ever wanted to expand your ministry beyond the galleys?

VINCENT
I want to be of service wherever God puts me, *Éminence*.

MAZARIN
And if he put you in the royal court? It wouldn't take much to have it arranged.

VINCENT
Merci, Éminence. You honor me. But my place is with the wretched. I'm most at home there. Besides, you were just mentioning the recent increase of disreputable people at court. Don't make a bad situation worse by inviting the likes of me to hang about.

Shouting from the king's chambers.

LOUIS
Mazarin! You worm!

ANNE
It doesn't hurt to have friends at court, *monsieur Vincent*. Even if you rarely visit.

VINCENT
I agree, my lady.

ANNE
Do me a favor: Reconsider our offer to stay the night. You need resources if your work is going to help as many as are in need of it. And we need a friend who has the confidence of the king. Perhaps, should God will it, we can benefit one another.

Mazarin enters the king's chambers.

MAZARIN
Majesté?

LOUIS
Yes. I've changed my mind. Send him in.
MAZARIN
The priest, my lord?

LOUIS
No, Pantagruel, King of the Dipsodes. Yes the priest, *ta mére la pute!*[8]

---

8 ... you son of a whore.

MAZARIN
Yes, my lord. Right away, my lord.

LOUIS
Wait, Mazarin.

MAZARIN
Yes, my lord?

LOUIS
See to it that I get my wine.

MAZARIN
Yes, my lord.

LOUIS
I want you to fetch it yourself and bring it to me. Don't send anyone else.

MAZARIN
Yes, my lord.

LOUIS
D'accord. Allons-y.

Mazarin opens the door.

ANNE
Remember what we were discussing. We can be good friends to one another.

VINCENT
My lady.

Vincent enters the King's chambers and Mazarin shuts the door.

MAZARIN
Your Highness.

LOUIS
What is it? What do you want?

MAZARIN
Your Highness, may I present monsieur Vincent de Paul.

LOUIS
I thought I told you I wanted to be left in peace, you damnable fool.

MAZARIN
Yes. Umm ...

VINCENT
I insisted on seeing you, *Majesté*, as my time for departure draws near.

LOUIS
Insisted on seeing me?

VINCENT
Yes, Your Highness.

LOUIS
Well. Take a seat.

MAZARIN
I'll leave you two to get acquainted. My liege.

LOUIS
Now just a minute, you odious carbuncle.

MAZARIN
Yes, my liege?

LOUIS
What did I ask of you?

MAZARIN
I . . . I'm not sure, my liege.

LOUIS
Plus de vin! Plus de vin! More wine, damn it! More wine!

MAZARIN
Yes, my liege. Yes. More wine. *Tout suite.*

Exit Mazarin.

LOUIS
So, you're St. Vincent?

VINCENT
I don't know what you've heard about me, *Majesté*.

LOUIS
S'il vous plait. Enough of this "*Majesté*" nonsense or I'll think you're a scoundrel like the rest of them.

VINCENT
Then no more "St. Vincent" either, or I'll think the
same of you.

LOUIS
Comme tu veux, monsieur Vincent.[9]

VINCENT
Why am I here?

LOUIS
They all think I'm an imbecile,
every damned one of them.

VINCENT
They do.

LOUIS
Well, what do you think?

VINCENT
I think it would be hard for an imbecile to occupy the
throne for three decades, especially such calamitous
decades as we've just lived through.

LOUIS
Continue.

VINCENT
I also think it can be advantageous for a wise man to
play the fool.

---

9   As you wish, monsieur Vincent.

LOUIS
Have you read Cassius Dio's *Historia Romana*? Do you know how Claudius became emperor, how he escaped the purges of Tiberius and Caligula?

VINCENT
I did once, but much of what I've known is now forgotten.

A knock at the door. Louis picks up a book and reads it upside down.

LOUIS
Entrez!

Enter Mazarin.

MAZARIN
I've brought the wine, *Majesté*. And a pair of clean chalices, in case *monsieur l'abbé* desires to join you.

LOUIS
Mazarin, you're a learned man.

MAZARIN
Yes, *Majesté*. I wouldn't be a worthy hand if I wasn't.

LOUIS
Then pray tell me what language this is. I don't even recognize the characters.

Mazarin turns the book right-side-up for the king.

MAZARIN
C'est anglais, Majesté.[10] These are the plays of William Shakespeare. You had me ask Sir Edward Herbert to bring you a copy when he visited from London.

LOUIS
Edward Herbert?

MAZARIN
The diplomat, *Majesté*. He used to be the English ambassador to your court.

LOUIS
Tell him when you see him that I prefer books with pictures.

MAZARIN
Oui en effet. Is there anything else?

LOUIS
Non, monseigneur. Tu peux aller.[11]

Exit Mazarin.

LOUIS
He'll be listening at the keyhole, the viper.
I take it the queen is out there as well?

VINCENT
She is.

LOUIS

---
10 It's English, Your Majesty.
11 No, monsignor. You can go.

That'll never do. Go tell them to leave.

VINCENT
To be honest, I think that directive is better coming from you.

LOUIS
Away from the door you leech! And take that faithless whore with you!

Mazarin and Anne hurry off.

Act II

II.1 *The king's chambers.*

VINCENT
I don't quite understand the purpose of this visit.

LOUIS
You know what bothers me most? The pretense. *Les mensonges.*[12] They told you I'm dying, I suppose. Or that I'm a fool for thinking I am.

VINCENT
They mentioned it.

LOUIS
Look at me. I've become a caricature: The aged monarch who everyone thinks is mad, wrestling with his mortality. I'm no better than a work of fiction. I belong in one of these god-cursed books!

VINCENT
Life is a book, no? With all of us playing our parts.

LOUIS
I see you've read some Shakespeare too.

VINCENT
I took the easy way out and read it right side up.

LOUIS
You know, I first heard of him because he wrote a play about one of my favorite characters in all of

---

12 The lies.

literature, the sad, desperate Cardenio from *Don Quixote*. Have you read it?

VINCENT
Which one?

LOUIS
Either?

VINCENT
I read Oudin's translation of *Quixote* years ago. I haven't read the play.

LOUIS
Oudin. Oudin was a good man. A good friend. A brilliant mind. Tell me, *mon père*, how is it that God can make good honest men like Oudin, only to allow them to suffer—and I mean suffer: the long, protracted suffering of illness and infirmity—and then sit by and watch them slowly succumb to the indignity of death?

VINCENT
Je ne sais pas.[13]

LOUIS
No. How could you? How could anyone make sense of that? So you've read the *Quixote*? Well, it's a popular book. What else do you like to read?

---

13   I don't know.

VINCENT
Not much these days. I barely have time to answer my correspondences. I'm afraid the life of the mind has passed me by.

LOUIS
But you can't let it atrophy. It's the one consolation we have.

VINCENT
I used to think so. Now I see it for what it is.

LOUIS
C'est quoi?

VINCENT
A means of attaining power, or else of pursuing pleasure—which really amounts to the same thing.

LOUIS
Ah. Spoken like one who's never had to rely on his faculties in order to survive. Oh! to be a priest. Would that I was a priest. What could be better?

A pause.

LOUIS
Allez. It isn't a rhetorical question. Tell me truly, what beats it?

VINCENT
I can think of a few things.

LOUIS
"Man is the animal that walks on two legs and is ungrateful," quoth a great anthropologist. You are too busy enjoying your fortune to appreciate it.

VINCENT
Is that so?

LOUIS
Absolument.

VINCENT
And what is the nature of these riches?

LOUIS
You have what everyone wants.

VINCENT
Which is?

LOUIS
Perpetual childhood. A man in a collar, whatever his age, is but a boy. Think on it. Your meals? Provided. Your lodgings? Secured. Your leisure? Sacred and unmolested as a tabernacle. Your enemy? The same and only enemy of every spoiled child. *L'ennui.*

VINCENT
It sounds as though you are describing a prisoner . . .
Or a king.

LOUIS
There is at least one salient difference. A child is a child because his father lives. A king is a king

because his father is dead. And a priest is a priest because his father cannot die. We would not tolerate him otherwise. A child of God. A child of eternity. The eternal child. I think I would have made a magnificent priest.

VINCENT
In my experience, the first wish of boys and the last wish of old men is to be a child no longer.

LOUIS
No, no. Their wish is to forget that they are children. A very important distinction. What they want—what we all want—is the strength and freedom and temerity to sin, without the consequences thereof.

VINCENT
What sin is without consequence?

LOUIS
Why, the sins of the priest, *mon père*. Not entirely, of course. He might get gout or the clap. But he will never get the rope or the rack. A great career!

VINCENT
Would you like me to make arrangements? You're welcome to join the Mission as a lay brother.

LOUIS
Sadly, no. That would be quite impossible for me. As you have seen, I am a born dissembler. Hypocrisy comes with my birth and my station as reliably as my scepter and my crown. But I'm afraid I'm too honest to take any of your vows.

VINCENT
Too honest?

LOUIS
Don't misunderstand me. I lie all the time. I make a sport, and if I may say, an art, of lying. The difference between the honest and the dishonest man, is that the honest man doesn't lie to himself.

VINCENT
I've yet to meet the man who doesn't lie to himself.

LOUIS
That's the first realization of an honest man—*il n'est honnête pas*.[14] My problem with you priests is not that you sin—that I can understand. It's not even that you get away with it—that I can admire. It's that you don't believe. The Black Death proved it. What did they do in Milan? Barred the doors to the churches. Heard confessions through wooden doors. Celebrated mass in empty streets while the faithful huddled safely by their windows.

VINCENT
They were trying to protect their flock.

LOUIS
They were trying to protect themselves.

---

14 —he is not honest.

VINCENT
The author of those policies, the Archbishop of Milan, administered the Eucharist to the sick throughout the plague, despite the protests of the government.

LOUIS
And he was so brave, so faithful, so exceptional, they made him a saint. Saint Charles Borromeo. And there was also a Saint Bridget of Sweden. And in an earlier plague, Saint Catherine of Sienna. But where were the rest of them? In hiding, like their Pope and their God.

VINCENT
More priests died than doctors. So many, in fact, that they effectively eliminated the qualifications for ordination.

LOUIS
God's judgment for their faithlessness, no doubt.

VINCENT
Or the natural consequence of tending to the sick and dying.

LOUIS
Allez, mon père. Allez. The pontifex maximus, the vicar of Christ, he who holds the keys that bind and loose eternally . . . left the city. He left the city. The very rock of the faith, rolling down into Campagna.

VINCENT
Yes, and St. Peter denied Christ.

LOUIS
He made up for that, though, didn't he? If every Pope's tenure ended with a crucifixion, there wouldn't be a single Protestant on the continent. Probably no Mohammedans either.

VINCENT
Or any Christians, if that kept up. It sounds like you're pining for Nero or Diocletian.

LOUIS
Those Roman despots built the church, whatever their actual intentions might have been. If you see one man choose to be crucified and lit on fire rather than offend his god, you can't help but believe he believes. If you watch a hundred men elect to become human lanterns, you can't help but believe yourself.

VINCENT
You are the king, after all. There is nothing stopping you from lighting your gardens however you see fit.

LOUIS
A futile enterprise. The Christians are the crucifiers now, mostly of each other. They've traded sack cloth for silk robes, sandals for slippers, martyrdom for murder.

VINCENT
Not every priest in France wears silk robes.

LOUIS
Every priest wants to, no matter what he tells himself or his mother. All except one, as I understand it.

Louis fills his glass with wine and raises it to Vincent.

LOUIS
Wine is a merry thing.

VINCENT
You don't look like you believe that.

LOUIS
"Give them bread to sustain them and wine to gladden their hearts." Isn't that what the Psalmist says?

VINCENT
You drink it as if it were medicine.

LOUIS
Well, I suppose I've always been more pagan than Christian at heart. "Great is the strength which generous wine imparts to wearied men." That's from Homer.

VINCENT
What makes you so weary? Perhaps you've read too many books?

LOUIS
Je suis vieux, mon père.[15] And dying.

---

15 I'm old, Father.

VINCENT
Not every old man loses the spark of life. Why hasten death's approach? Impatience is the meanest form of ingratitude, as you well know.

LOUIS
Yes, ingratitude. I mentioned that before. It is man's original sin. But then, what has God given us to be so grateful about? Death? War? Plague? Infirmity? Malice? Stupidity? Greed? No. I've seen too much of life to ever feel grateful for it. God made the mistake of letting me live too long.

VINCENT
More than a few would consider that mistake a blessing.

LOUIS
Ah, so now we're taking advice from the many? Yes, the people understand what's in their interest. They discern it with the wisdom of the fool.

VINCENT
Remind me, O Doctor of the Church, who it was that said wisdom can be found in folly? St. Paul, was it not?

LOUIS
A fool himself, as far as I'm concerned. One who confused strength for vice and servitude for humility. Speaking of which, did you see I have a knave?

VINCENT
I did.

LOUIS
He's a rogue, isn't he? God, I love him. My favorite pet.

VINCENT
His Eminence doesn't seem to share your enthusiasm.

LOUIS
Well, the Mazarins of the world wouldn't, would they? They don't understand anything. Do you know what made me want one?

VINCENT
A fool? Let me guess. Something you read?

LOUIS
Don't tell me I'm becoming predictable, Father. *Tout sauf ça!*[16] There's no greater sin. To be predictable is to be dead, or to invite your enemies to kill you.

VINCENT
Then surprise me. Why bring a fop to the royal court?

LOUIS
It was the story of Triboulet. Have you heard of him?

VINCENT
I can't say I have.

LOUIS
He was the great jester who lived in the court of Francis I. He was born with an unusually small head

---

16 Anything but that!

(the size of a coconut, they say), and he used it to his advantage. No one had more license with the king.

VINCENT
And no one more bondage if he was seen, as you see your fool, as a pet and not a man.

LOUIS
Ah, but men treat their pets better than their fellow men, don't they? My dogs are washed, fed, groomed, pampered. They sleep on finer beds than any peasant in the kingdom. Who treats man so well? Only a true buffoon would deign to scrub the filth from another human being.

VINCENT
People beat their pets, do they not?

LOUIS
To train them, yes. But that's the thing. Animals will be trained. Man, on the other hand, is a stubborn beast. He refuses domestication.

VINCENT
Obedience is a challenging virtue. But the human heart is not so wild that, given a good and loving master, it can't learn to obey.

LOUIS
Encore une erreur, mon père.[17] Those pious sentiments may satisfy the feeble old widows that fill out your pews, but the church herself knows better. She never

---

17 Another mistake, Father.

tires of teaching humility. The proud, she says, will be chastened. If not in this world, then in the next. So, you see, I'm only following the church's lead when I say that man cannot be tamed. He must either be broken or put to death. That is the choice left the crown.

VINCENT
The church is the last refuge for those broken by the crown, a source of comfort to the dying.

LOUIS
A fool's comfort, if ever there was one. What comfort does the church have to offer? The promise of eternal punishment for one's enemies? In that way, she's like the king who told Triboulet that if anyone killed him, the offender would be put to death 15 minutes later. "I'd rather it were 15 minutes before," the fool said in reply. Even he saw the emptiness of such solace.

VINCENT
I'm not sure I've met a theologian who holds eternal damnation to be one of the church's chief consolations.

LOUIS
Ah, how little its defenders understand the appeal of the institution they claim to represent. Why be good if there's no reward in the end? And a reward is only a reward if others can't have it.

VINCENT
Now who's offering a fool's wisdom?

LOUIS
Am I? I'd call it the wisdom of the world. But perhaps your friend Paul was onto something after all. He certainly didn't stick around to die of old age.

VINCENT
I seem to remember him advising against drunkenness too.

LOUIS
I suppose we'll both have some explaining to do when we meet him.

VINCENT
Paul understood that a life awaits us beyond this life. He could see through the veil of earthly pleasures.

LOUIS
The thing about pleasure, *mon père*, is that it's always bound up with pain. Anyone claiming to seek release from the one is usually running from the other.

VINCENT
There is no escaping pain. Not in this life, anyway. Suffering is its essence.

LOUIS
A lesson they'd do well to emphasize in catechesis. Do you want to hear another story about our friend Triboulet? He once made bold to slap Francis on the ass. (Imagine taking such liberty with a king!) Embarrassed, Francis was ready to have him run through with swords, but he told the fool he'd offer

him clemency if he could come up with an apology more insulting than the insult.

VINCENT
What did Triboulet say?

LOUIS
He said he'd mistaken the king for the queen and grabbed his ass intending to grab hers.
Now there's a fool!

VINCENT
How did Francis take it?

LOUIS
How do you think? He sentenced him to death. But, out of love for his clown—for he really did love him, the way one loves a favorite commode—he offered to let Triboulet choose how he would die. And do you know what he said, fool that he was?

VINCENT
Old age?

LOUIS
Old age! *Espèce de coquin!*[18] You do know the story.

VINCENT
I may have read it years ago.

---

18 You rascal!

LOUIS
Voila. That's the wisdom of a fool. And you, apparently, share it as well!

VINCENT
There are worse ways to die.

LOUIS
Spoken like a man too far removed from infirmity to understand its horrors. But let me tell you, *mon père*, as one who knows, there is no more agonizing death than to live too long. Better to be hanged, drawn, and quartered than to sit and count the grains of sand as they fall from the hourglass.

II.2 *Château ballroom. Mazarin and Anne observe the revelers and Fool.*

MAZARIN
They've been in there for hours.

ANNE
How do you read it? *C'est bon ou mal?*[19]

MAZARIN
Never trust a man of the cloth. That's the first rule of politics.

ANNE
And yet, you'd have me trust you.

---

19 Is it good or bad?

MAZARIN
Well, my lady, I don't see you having much choice.

Enter Servant.

SERVANT
Éminence. Majesté.

MAZARIN
What is it?

SERVANT
His Majesty asks for you, Your Eminence.

MAZARIN
He does? Did he say what he wants?
SERVANT
Oui, Éminence.

MAZARIN
Alors? Crache-le déjà, garçon.[20] Don't make me get the torturers to pry it from you.

SERVANT
Plus du vin, Éminence.

MAZARIN
Is that all?

SERVANT
Oui, Éminence.

---

20 So? Spit it out, boy.

MAZARIN
Allons-y. I'll attend to His Majesty as soon as I'm able.

SERVANT
Oui, Éminence.

Exit Servant.

MAZARIN
"He wants more wine." I should drown him in wine!

ANNE
Jules.

MAZARIN
He's like some tyrant out of a Greek tragedy. *C'est un fléau.*[21] He's a plague upon this land, upon its people, upon you and upon me.

ANNE
We must be careful, not just in what we say but most especially in what we do. A sick man is not a sane man. And I don't want to end up like his mother.

MAZARIN
Jamais. You won't end up like her. I'll see to that.

ANNE
We must be careful, Jules. He sent her into exile and had her closest advisors rounded up and executed. That's not a fate I want for either of us.

---

21 It's a scourge.

MAZARIN
And how would you write our fates, my lady?

ANNE
Intertwined. As we've imagined.

MAZARIN
You as regent during young Louis' minority.

ANNE
And you as de facto king.

MAZARIN
I don't trust that damned priest.
ANNE
Vincent?

MAZARIN
Yes. Vincent. Anyone with a reputation like his is hiding something.

ANNE
Perhaps he really is a holy man. I've always thought so.

MAZARIN
No. What are you hoping to get out of him anyway?

ANNE
Direction.

MAZARIN
On?

ANNE
How to be a fit mother for a king.

MAZARIN
You're expecting to learn that from him?

ANNE
There's something about him. *Je ne sais quoi . . . quelque chose . . . gentile.*[22]

MAZARIN
What's he been doing in there all this time? What's he been telling our king?

II.3 *The king's chambers. Louis and Vincent converse.*

LOUIS
I'm surrounded by vipers. That's what it is to be king. Alone in a den of vipers.

VINCENT
That's what it is to be any man.

LOUIS
No. Wearing the crown is different. It robs you of the luxury of trifles.

VINCENT
I know you know your Roman history. Do you remember the cause of the Perusine War? Fulvia wanted Augustus to *couché avec elle* to get revenge for

---

22 I don't know what . . . something . . . gentile.

Antony's infidelity. She threatened to start a war if he refused. Do you remember Augustus' reply?

LOUIS
"Doesn't she know that my prick is dearer to me than my life? Sound the trumpets of war!"

VINCENT
It seems to me that the trifles of kings are the causes of great sorrow for others.

LOUIS
Bravo, mon père! I knew I was a bad influence, but I never would have imagined I could get a living saint to spew such impieties.

VINCENT
There's nothing impious about telling the truth.

LOUIS
Quid est veritas?[23]

VINCENT
Truth is the word heard only by those who listen.

LOUIS
Sophisme! Sophism of the highest degree! And here I thought I was discussing truth with a cleric.

VINCENT
Tell me. What will happen to your son when you die? He's very young. Only just a boy.

---

23 What is truth?

LOUIS
I was a boy when I became king.

VINCENT
How old?

LOUIS
It was before my ninth birthday.

VINCENT
That's a heavy burden to place on so small a brow.

LOUIS
I managed.

VINCENT
How?

LOUIS
I did what I had to.

VINCENT
And what was that, Majesty?

A knock at the door.

VINCENT
Why did you ask me here? What do you want from me?

Enter Mazarin.

LOUIS
Quoi?! Que veux-tu?![24]

MAZARIN
You sent for me, Majesty?

LOUIS
Yes. I wanted to tell you what a sot you are. And what a rat-faced weasel. You think yourself clever but, as Father Vincent and I were just discussing, your pride will be your downfall. It will lead you right to the scaffold if you don't watch out. Now where's my wine?

Mazarin walks over and places a full jug before him.

LOUIS
Nothing to say?

MAZARIN
I live at your pleasure, Majesty. And at the pleasure of your friends.

LOUIS
Get out of my sight, whoremonger.

MAZARIN
Bien sûr, Majesté.

Exit Mazarin.

VINCENT
Why do you abuse him so?

---

24 What?! What do you want?!

LOUIS
There's such little happiness in this life. One must enjoy it when one finds it.

VINCENT
It's a mean sort of happiness.

LOUIS
What sort of happiness isn't? Even the things you relish—prayer, let's say, and self-denial—smack of cruelty. Some pleasures are bought by abusing others. Some by abusing oneself. I have an appetite for both. Except instead of spending my days debasing myself and my nights crippling my knees in prayer, I mortify my flesh with wine. Drunkenness is a kind of self-flagellation. A form of penance, if you will.

VINCENT
A form of penance that falls on deaf ears.

LOUIS
As all penance does, *mon père*. As all penance does.

VINCENT
Something in me suspects that I'm not really here for you.

LOUIS
You've spent quite a lot of time talking to someone you're not here to see.

VINCENT
I was told you wanted to make a confession.

LOUIS
What do you call this?

VINCENT
A trial.

LOUIS
Believe me, *mon père*, if I were putting you on trial, it would be a lot less pleasant. Besides, being king means not having to get my hands dirty. I have men who handle that sort of business for me.

VINCENT
The confession was a pretense to get me in the door.
LOUIS
Why would I need one?

VINCENT
You knew I wouldn't come otherwise. I've already turned down several of the queen's invitations. I'm too busy with my work.

LOUIS
And what would I want that necessitates such a ruse?

VINCENT
You wanted to examine me for yourself.

LOUIS
Why, pray tell, would I want to do that?

VINCENT
What will happen to your son when you're dead?

LOUIS
Je ne sais pas. Who can tell a man what will be after him under the sun?

VINCENT
Save your insouciance, Majesty. There isn't time, and there isn't anything else for you to think about now.

LOUIS
Soyez prudent, mon père.[25] You're talking to your king.

A stare. A drink.
LOUIS
It took 23 years to get him. I'm an old man now. I wasn't when we first wed. But she had four stillbirths. Four. I didn't know if I'd ever have an heir. I prayed and I prayed and eventually I stopped praying. Then he came, all of a sudden, like a ray from the sun breaking in after decades of dark. And now I'm dying. *C'est la vie.*

VINCENT
A father can only do so much.

LOUIS
But isn't that the sin of it all? When he's here, your father is an obstacle. A tyrant who must be overcome. And when he's gone—well, his absence makes matters all the worse. He's the god you can't quite get rid of. And a wretched god at that.

---

25 Careful, Father.

VINCENT
It's not too late for you to do what your father never could.

LOUIS
What's that?

VINCENT
Ask for the boy's forgiveness.

LOUIS
For what?

VINCENT
For what he must suffer on your account.

LOUIS
It's no more than I have suffered. And I'm not trying to die, whatever you may think of my habits. Not, in any case, more than anyone else. Certainly not more than you when you peck your lepers and whatever else you saints do.

VINCENT
Alors qui est à blâmer?[26]

LOUIS
The inscrutable humors, the greater or maybe the lesser bear, my father and his father and his father's father, Clovis and Charlamagne and all the Carolingian kings, Adam himself. If I could answer

---

26 So who is to blame?

that question, what need would I or anyone else have of you?

VINCENT
What need do you have of me now?

LOUIS
Franchement, mon père, it is neither my sins nor my son's pity that I am interested in this evening. Still less your apologies and evasions.

VINCENT
Perhaps, then, I should go.

LOUIS
You will leave when I dismiss you. If I decide to dismiss you.

Silence.

LOUIS
Saint Vincent. People really call you that, you know. Aren't you humiliated?

VINCENT
I try not to think about it.

LOUIS
I suppose I wouldn't want to either. Correct me if I am wrong, but you come from a very poor family, do you not?

VINCENT
We had plenty.

LOUIS
You didn't even have shoes.

VINCENT
And still, I stand before the king of France.

LOUIS
Voici! There's the pride I've been looking for. That's how you crawled out of that little hovel and shook its dust from your feet. Oh, don't pull a face now. I admire it. *C'est vrai.*[27] You were *trop intelligent, trop exceptional, trop brillant,* to die like your father, spade in hand, in someone else's field. So, you didn't. You became the youngest priest in Christendom. Nineteen years old, weren't you? There was a special dispensation from Rome, was there not? And then there was Paris and the academic distinction and the bored, solicitous, rich old women. "*L'abbé*, Madame Jolie left you this exquisite chaise." "*L'abbé*, Madame LeClerc is bringing you a closet of silk suits."
Mon Dieu, you could have been Cardinal.
Peut-être un père, qui sait?[28]

VINCENT
I'm still ashamed.

LOUIS
Non, mon père, non. Au contraire. This is the man I wanted to meet. This is the man I still hope to meet. This man is not a man. He is a god. No, don't scoff. I won't allow it. What is God but the *causa sui*? You made yourself out of nothing. And what nothing is

---

27 It is true.
28 Maybe a father, who knows?

more obscure and fathomless than those ciphers that
make our bread?

VINCENT
You mock me.

LOUIS
Pas de tout, mon semblable, mon idéal.[29] What do
you think made Zeus the king of Olympus? The
thunderbolts? Even the English have those. No, it
was the stone he snuck in Cronos' gullet, or rather,
les pierres to be a parricide. I've heard—please tell
me I've heard truly—that your father came to visit
you at the University in Toulouse. God knows how
he got there, in those rags, with that limp. Somehow,
he gets all the way there. Lingers awkwardly, one
must imagine, by the threshold, smelling like a dung
heap. He finally summons the courage (or was it
pride? pride in his brilliant son) to ask for you. Word
winds its way through the corridors. You hear, you
pause, you look down from the parapet of your ivory
tower at your shame, and you turn your back. You
don't even tell him that you're not coming. How long,
I wonder, did he wait for his son? How long did he
stand there before he departed?

VINCENT
C'est vrai.

LOUIS
I don't judge you. Not for this. You were pitiless. Yes.
Cruel, even. *Mais tu étais honnête.*[30] You would not

---
29 Not at all, my likeness, my ideal.
30 But you were honest.

pretend that that ... fragment was your father any longer. You no longer had a father—you didn't lose him, like I lost mine, and my son will lose his. You exiled him to Tartarus. I had no such opportunity, and I doubt very much if I ever would have had the courage.

VINCENT
It was the basest cowardice.

LOUIS
No, the cowardice came later. The histrionic denial of your achievements. The surrender of your station. Playing nursemaid to galley slaves and half men like your father. Giving up your silk robes for their stink. That was cowardice. And I have to know how it happened. What—or maybe who—made you betray yourself? *J'exige de savoir.*[31] Was there a voice? Was there a vision? Did you go blind riding your horse towards Damascus? Did you wake up one morning with a blister *sur ton dard?*[32]

A glare. A sip.

LOUIS
Don't try to tell me the pirate story is true. Some barbary corsairs snatched you up in raid off Marseilles and sold you to some Tunisian Mohammedans? Made you into a manservant, did they, for a few long years? Some missionaries bought you back, and you left your taste for luxury with the tawny princes of Africa? *S'il vous plait.* It's a

---
31 I demand to know.
32 ... on your Christopher?

plagiarism and an absurdity. Who are you supposed to be, Caesar?

VINCENT
Those damned letters.

LOUIS
Ne vous inquiétez pas.[33] No one could possibly believe them. Still the question remains. I know frauds like you know the indigent. They never leave me for a moment. They dress me and advise me and attend me at my close stool. I knew you were a fraud from the moment I heard about your exploits, about your miraculous conversion. And now that I met you, "beard to beard," as the Bard would say, I also know that you have a deep disgust for yourself. (I too am repulsed by my reflection.) *Confesser, mon père.* Disburden your soul.

---

33   Don't worry.

… Act III

III.1 *Flashback. Churchyard. Enter Sextants.*

FIRST SEXTANT
Merde! A half-hour's walk I have in this. I'll be lucky to keep half my toes.

He notices a small wooden box, covered in a blanket. He bends down and reaches inside.

SECOND SEXTANT
Mort.

FIRST SEXTANT
You don't say, doctor. They might as well throw them in the river.

SECOND SEXTANT
Some do.

FIRST SEXTANT
Only the honest ones. *A bientôt.*

Exeunt sextants. Enter Vincent and a young woman who drops a basket next to the box and hurries away.

VINCENT
Qu'est-ce que vous fait?[34]

Exit young woman.

VINCENT
Attendre! S'il vous plaît! Madame!

---

34 What are you doing?

A voice from the shadows.

BEGGAR
They don't hold on for very long this time of year.
The other one was there for two hours or so. I thought
he'd never stop crying. But he did.

VINCENT
And you just sat here?

BEGGAR
Je n'avais pas le choix.[35] I don't have legs. Not easy to
carry a baby when you walk on your hands.

VINCENT
Are many babies left here like this?

BEGGAR
Three, four a day, I'd say. Half die of the cold.
The other half wish they had.

VINCENT
Pourquoi?

BEGGAR
They get sold to beggars like me who maim them.
Broken babies bring lots of money. Whole babies,
not so much. And broken men . . . Pah! . . . Hardly
anything at all.

VINCENT
Do their mothers know what happens to them?

---

35   I had no choice.

BEGGAR
I doubt it. Though I doubt they try very hard to find out.

Silence.

BEGGAR
I don't judge them. Better not to know these things. *Tu n'es pas d'accord, mon père?*[36]

III.2 *Flashback. Estate dining room. Madame LeClerc, Madame de Gondi, and a group of women. Vincent.*

MADAME LECLERC
Monsieur Vincent, we have spoken our minds with all possible honesty and charity. And common sense. Women know what is and what is not possible. Among the weakness and the misery that God has given us, we have that at least. You men wouldn't make so many mistakes if you just listened to us for once.

MADAME DE GONDI
Madame ...

MADAME LECLERC
I didn't mean what I said, Sir. *Je suis tellement désolée.*[37]

---

36 Don't you agree, Father?
37 I'm very sorry.

VINCENT
No, I agree, Madame Leclerc. I am glad sometimes that I lack common sense. Common sense leads us to many sins.

NOBLE WOMAN TWO
Monsieur l'abbé, we need your answer.

Vincent opens his cloak, takes out a baby, and places him on the table.

MADAME DE GONDI
Qu'est-ce que c'est ça?[38]
VINCENT
My answer. You think I do too much. I think I'm not doing enough. Go to any church in this city, and you will find three or four children left to die every night.

MADAME LECLERC
Maybe God wants them to die. They are, after all, children of sin.

VINCENT
When God wants someone to die for sins, he sends his son. God never wanted a single innocent child to pay for sin. It is the cowardly, the selfish, and the vicious who accept that.

MADAME LECLERC
Monsieur l'abbé, I respect you, but I won't follow you blindly. I hate sin and vice. And this child is the rotten fruit of sin and vice.

---

38 What is this?

VINCENT
God is listening to you, Madame.

MADAME LECLERC
God cannot possibly love him.

VINCENT
I will not let you be the judge of that. I know that God is asking me to save this innocent child before anyone else. I will go out tomorrow and every night, and I will put more on this table. You will watch them fight and ask you to help them live. We will see if you let them die.

NOBLE WOMAN TWO
Monsieur l'abbé, we have told you that we have too much on our hands. I know you think we are merely rich and idle women. But we work day and night, no less than the fishmongers. Ask any woman here and she will tell you, *nous ne pouvons plus rein faire.*[39]

VINCENT
There is more to be done.

NOBLE WOMAN TWO
We are trying to talk reasonably.

VINCENT
I am the one who told you not to go too fast. But tonight, I'm afraid I've gone too slow.

---

39   . . . we can't do any more.

MADAME LECLERC
Monsieur l'abbé, there are institutions that collect
these children. They pay nurses to feed them.
Vous ne savez pas?[10]

VINCENT
I don't know what they do for children, but I know
that if I hadn't been there tonight, this child would be
lying in a basket in front of the church. And he would
be dead.

NOBLE WOMAN THREE
We have enough enemies, *monsieur l'abbé*. Priests
and judges are in charge of that work, and if we start
doing their jobs for them, they will hate us too.
VINCENT
I only know one judge.

MADAME LECLERC
You do as you wish. But I know that none of these
women will stain their hands taking care of these
miserable children and touch their own children
later. That would be a sin. And a grievous one at that.

MADAME DE GONDI
Please don't ask us for more. *S'il vous plait, monsieur
Vincent.* Think of what we have given. *S'il vous plait.*
Don't ask for too much.

MADAME DE GONDI
What you want to do here is too repugnant.

---

40 Don't you know?

VINCENT
So are you. All of you. Look at me. Look at this child. Madame?

NOBLE WOMAN ONE
I'm ashamed, but it disgusts me.

VINCENT
Et toi?

NOBLE WOMAN FOUR
I have children of my own.

VINCENT
Toi aussi?

NOBLE WOMAN FIVE
God's judgment is just.

VINCENT
I was a fool to believe I could move your souls, that I could free you from your repulsive solitude. This child is here for you. I brought him here. I brought him here, and he is here for you. *Pour toi. Vous ne comprenez pas?*[41] Here is your salvation. There is no other. Look at him. Look at him and you will see. *Il est un enfant. S'il vous plait.* He's only a child. Please just look at him.

---

41   For you. Don't you understand?

III.3 *Present. The king's chambers. Louis and Vincent.*

LOUIS
D'accord, mon père. If you won't make a good confession. I will. *Je ne crois pas.*[42]

VINCENT
Is that supposed to be some kind of revelation?

LOUIS
I'm serious. Serious as the marble tomb being chiseled for me as we speak. I don't believe in God.

VINCENT
Most people don't.

LOUIS
In Catholic France?

VINCENT
If they believed, they'd live differently.

LOUIS
I disagree. Most believe. They need to believe. They're too afraid not to. But I don't have the luxury of their fear.

VINCENT
No?

---

42 I don't believe.

LOUIS
No. And my disbelief does not stem from the typical, trite arguments either.

VINCENT
You have enlightened reasons.

LOUIS
J'ai de meilleures raisons.[43] It's not that the wicked prosper and the innocent are slaughtered, that just men lose their heads and tyrants die in their sleep, sprawled out next to their child brides. I've seen too much to care for such trifles. And besides, one can always come up with excuses for those.

VINCENT
Why then?

LOUIS
You believe in Christ Jesus? The only begotten son of God Almighty. Second person of the Trinity. Sent to die for our sins.

VINCENT
Je fais.

LOUIS
But what does that mean, Father? What did I just say? I said certain words, in a certain order. But did I say anything at all?

---

43 I have better reasons.

VINCENT
You said the most consequential words that can be said.

LOUIS
Non, je dis rein. I said that God became man, that He who cannot die and was not born—who cannot even change, such is His perfection—became a helpless suckling, a defecating, snot-ridden child. I said that the Creator of the cosmos, the author of the heavens and the stars, ate and shat and died the death of a slave.

VINCENT
Oui.

LOUIS
C'est absurde. That's more than absurd. It defies belief.

VINCENT
No one has ever disputed that.

LOUIS
No. No. Spare me the *credo quia absurdum*. I misspoke. It's not just absurd. It is quite literally unthinkable. It's no different than believing in a triangle with four sides.

VINCENT
"Thou hast hid these things from the wise and hast revealed them to the little ones."

LOUIS
Has he hid them from coherence too?

VINCENT
That's not your objection. You're still playing a part.

LOUIS
You're right. It's not my objection. Who is coherent? Who would want to be? I don't have an objection. I have a proof.

VINCENT
A proof?

LOUIS
Yes, for the non-existence of God. Would you like to hear it?

VINCENT
If I must.

LOUIS
Je suis ton roi.[44]

VINCENT
Alors continuez, Votre Majesté.

LOUIS
It's not suffering or logic that disproves God's existence. It's happiness. Blessed are the meek and the mournful and the poor indeed—for they do not know happiness.

VINCENT
This again?

---

44 I am your king.

LOUIS
Ah, I can see by your irritation that you know where I'm going. The terrible truth about human beings is that we can get used to anything. That's our great gift and our greater curse. Lepers get used to their sores and their shame as kings get used to their crowns and their concubines. And the lepers have the better of it. At least they can hope that maybe one day they will be cured. The king knows there are no cures. Every pleasure, every triumph, every joy will, in time, lose its savor.

VINCENT
In this life perhaps.

LOUIS
In any life. *Tu ne vois pas?*[45] If there were a heaven and a hell, there would be no difference between them. The punishment would be the same. The tyrant boiling in blood and the martyr looking out over heaven's ivory battlements would eventually be indistinguishable. In time, both would wish to die a true death.

VINCENT
You're playing games and I'm tired. I ought to be going. I have real work to attend to.

LOUIS
Je ne ris pas, mon père.[46] And I'm only telling you what you already know. What is happiness really? It's a beggar enjoying a warm meal after a night in the

---
45 Don't you see?
46 I'm not laughing, Father.

cold. It's the desperate gratitude in his eyes when you hand him that pan of thin gruel. Take away the cold and the poverty and the indifference of the world, and where would it go? Where would you find it?

VINCENT
You cannot think your way to happiness or to Christ. It's useless to try.

LOUIS
Then this whole evening has been useless.

VINCENT
I quite agree.

Silence.

LOUIS
Look out there. Watch the snowflakes as they're devoured by those pristine banks. They fall from one white oblivion to another. And when they land, they don't make a sound.

VINCENT
Did you really think I could make you believe?

LOUIS
Non, bien sûr que non.[47] I hoped you could, like an idiot child, like a condemned man in a tumbril.

Silence.

---

47   Of course not.

LOUIS

When I was a boy, my governess told me a silly little lie that has never left me. Nothing has ever dislodged it. It was the stroke of midnight on Christmas Eve, and she said to me, "Do you know my child, at this very moment, those majestic stallions that your father rides, Diomedes and Sarpedon, horses that only two men can even touch, and only one man has ever rode, they are kneeling in their strawy pens. Right now. For they too are waiting for the Christ child." I was delighted with that. I can still feel the thrill of it. (Children are such perfect idiots, *ne sont-ils pas?*) And yet, if you came to me this Christmas Eve, and said, "Come, let's see your Majesty's horses kneel to their true king," I would crawl off this chair and follow you into the cold, hoping it might be so.

Prolonged silence.

LOUIS

Thank you for your patience this evening, *mon père*. I'm sorry for wasting your time. Leave me. Return to your work. *Allez.*

Close curtains.

Epilogue

Epilogue. Courtyard. Vincent prepares to depart. Enter the queen.

ANNE
Monsieur Vincent! Monsieur.

VINCENT
Majesté.

ANNE
You're leaving?

VINCENT
I have to go.

ANNE
Ce qui s'est passe?[18] Did he send you away like all the others?

VINCENT
I have to go, my lady.

ANNE
Is he beyond saving, *monsieur Vincent?* Is he beyond hope?

VINCENT
If he can't be saved, none of us can.

ANNE
Will you come back to court? Will you help guide the Dauphin?

---

18   What happened?

VINCENT
It's nearly dawn. I must go.

ANNE
Ce qui s'est passe le nuit dernière?[49] What did he say?

VINCENT
He made his confession. He made a good confession.

Fin.

---

49   What happened last night?

A Word from the Editor-in-Chief

We at Senex Press would like to express our deepest gratitude to the Panteleimon Trithemius Literary Endowment for the generous gift that made the compilation and production of this play possible. For nearly 50 years, the Panteleimon Trithemius Literary Endowment has fostered works of great beauty, merit, and cultural significance, works that have otherwise been overlooked by the literary establishment and ignored by a nearly illiterate reading public. True to the spirit of Panteleimon Trithemius's incredible life and legacy, this text strives to provide readers with an encounter with an extraordinary character, one who, like Trithemius himself, has been all but forgotten. Martin Thrush may not have been a natural heir to Trithemius—who could claim so vaunted a mantle?—but he is certainly his beneficiary, in that a small fraction of the money Trithemius bequeathed his charitable fund went toward offsetting the nominal costs of typesetting this book. For that gift, and for Trithemius's vision, foresight, and example, we at Senex Press are sincerely grateful.

Jamieson de Quincey
Editor-in-Chief, Senex Press

Panteleimon Trithemius Literary Endowment

CREATION. INNOVATION. INSPIRATION.

www.ingramcontent.com/pod-product-compliance
Lightning Source LLC
Chambersburg PA
CBHW020554030426
42337CB00013B/1088